Inspiring Change: Elizabeth Fry

T0337811

Written by Donna David

Illustrated by Alice Negri

Contents

Collins

1 Elizabeth Fry's early life

Birth and childhood

Elizabeth Fry was born in Norwich, England in 1780. You might not have heard of her, but you may have seen her face printed on Bank of England five pound notes. Her work on prison reform was so important that we still see her ideas used in prisons today, over 200 years later.

Elizabeth Fry

Before she was married, Elizabeth Fry was named Elizabeth Gurney. Her family was extremely wealthy; her father owned a **spinning** factory and a banking business, and Elizabeth's mother, Catherine, raised their 12 children in their family home, Earlham Hall.

Earlham Hall

Women's rights in the 1700s

Life for women in the UK in the 1700s was very different to now. Women were expected to be wives and mothers, and the lessons they took in school reflected this. Their husbands or fathers were in charge of all decisions and, often, women didn't have their own money. Women couldn't vote or go to university, and married women weren't allowed to own land.

Quakers

The Gurney family were Quakers. Unusually for the time, Quakers believed that men and women were equal. This meant that, as well as learning sewing and household management, Elizabeth was taught Latin, French and Maths.

What is Quakerism?

Quakers are Christian members of a group called the Society of Friends. Quakers believe that there is good in everyone and that violence should always be avoided. The society was founded in England in the 17th century by George Fox.

To worship, Quakers gather in a group in a meeting room or in a house. The meeting can be completely silent until someone feels a need or urge to speak.

The makeshift school

As a teenager, there were hints at what Elizabeth might go on to do. She turned a disused room at the family home into a makeshift school and she invited poorer children who lived nearby to attend. Elizabeth enjoyed spending time with the children and teaching them how to read.

By this time, Elizabeth's mother had died but her father was very proud of his daughter's charity work and would bring his friends to the school to watch Elizabeth teach.

Molly Norman

As a teenager, Elizabeth spent a lot of her time helping the poor people who lived nearby. One day, Elizabeth met a girl of her own age, Molly Norman, in the park. After talking for a while, Elizabeth offered Molly a job. Elizabeth employed Molly and paid her out of her own pocket. Molly joined Elizabeth's school and became Elizabeth's maid.

Elizabeth's wealth

Elizabeth had a very different life to Molly and her other students. Elizabeth spent time with other rich families, and the difference between her life and the life of her students would have been very obvious. But Elizabeth made the most of having wealthy friends. She regularly asked them to donate clothes and blankets to distribute to families in need.

William Savery

One of the most important things to happen to Elizabeth as a teenager was hearing William Savery (an American Quaker) speak at a meeting. William Savery had travelled all over the world talking and preaching to other Quakers and, in 1798, he was in England. Elizabeth's whole family were excited to meet him.

When William Savery stood up and talked to the room, Elizabeth was transfixed. Savery spoke of his dislike of war and his belief in human kindness.

Elizabeth's diaries

Throughout her life, Elizabeth Fry kept a detailed diary. These diaries show that Elizabeth found spelling difficult, and historians think she may have had **dyslexia**. Nevertheless, she wrote in her diary almost every day.

In one extract from her diaries, Elizabeth described talking to William Savery for the first time:

"... we had much serious talk and what he said to me was like a refreshing shower on parched up earth ..."

Joseph Fry

Elizabeth was incredibly interested in William Savery's words, and the meeting made her determined to spend her time trying to improve the lives of the poor. Elizabeth wanted to be a "good Quaker" who put the needs of others before her own. Her family, who were less strict with their Quakerism, soon realised that Elizabeth was serious in her decision. When a **Plain Quaker**, Joseph Fry, asked Elizabeth to marry him, her father thought it was a good match.

The long proposal!

Elizabeth was allowed to make her own mind up about who she married which was very unusual for the time. Elizabeth met Joseph Fry and spent a year getting to know him. She liked Joseph, but not enough to marry him. He proposed in 1799 but she said no, and she didn't agree to marry him until almost a year later. In the early 1800s, women were expected to do as their husbands wished, but Joseph allowed his wife to make her own decisions which enabled her to focus on her work throughout their marriage.

Joseph and Elizabeth Fry were married in 1800 and moved to Joseph's family home, Plashet House in London. In 1800, Plashet House was in the countryside. However, if we were to visit the same spot now, we would find a busy neighbourhood just 13 kilometres from central London.

In her new home, Elizabeth missed her family terribly. To begin with, she found married life difficult and boring. Elizabeth's new mother-in-law only wanted to talk about her clothes or various illnesses. Elizabeth longed for something to do and was desperate for interesting and challenging work.

2 Newgate Prison

Life in London

By 1812, Joseph and Elizabeth had eight children (they would eventually have 11 children in total). The family now spent a lot of time at their house in London, where newspapers estimated that over 1000 people were starving to death every day. Elizabeth saw first-hand how very poor people were living in the city.

The Industrial Revolution

In the early 1800s, the Industrial Revolution was underway. Machines were being used in factories for the first time. This left many people unemployed because the machines were doing the jobs people used to do by hand.

The Watt steam engine was one machine that was used in factories.

Food prices

While Elizabeth and her family were living in London, there was a series of bad harvests. This made the price of bread extremely expensive because there wasn't enough to go around.

With so many people out of work and with food being so expensive, the rate of crime in London was on the rise. More people than ever were being sent to prison, even for the smallest of crimes, stealing bread being one of them.

Visiting Newgate Prison

In 1813, a Quaker man named Stephen Grellet was travelling around the UK, visiting the sick and poor. He visited Newgate Prison in London and was shocked by the conditions he saw. Prisoners were asleep on the floor. They had no mattresses or blankets, just a scattering of straw. There were no washing facilities, so prisoners were often very dirty and unwell. If a mother was sent to prison, then her children went in with her. Babies and toddlers were running around overcrowded prison cells which they shared with serious and violent criminals.

Newgate Prison

Time to help

On leaving Newgate Prison, Stephen Grellet called together
a group of Quaker Friends and asked for their help.
They immediately set to work. Elizabeth Fry was one of
the Friends and she quickly gathered clothes and blankets and,
the very next day, she went to Newgate Prison.

Prison conditions

To begin with, the governor of Newgate Prison wouldn't let Elizabeth in, but she insisted. When she was eventually allowed inside, she was shocked and saddened by what she saw.

On 13th February 1813, Elizabeth sent a letter to her children about what she'd seen:

"I have lately been twice to Newgate to see after the poor prisoners who had poor little infants without clothing, or with very little and I think if you saw how small a piece of bread they are each allowed a day you would be very sorry."

16

Elizabeth Fry got straight to work. She dressed every baby and handed out blankets to the prisoners. She returned the next day, and the day after that, with more clothes, blankets and fresh straw for the prisoners.

Hungry prisoners

The more Elizabeth Fry visited Newgate Prison, the more distressed she was to learn what life was like for the inmates. At this time, prison guards were unpaid. They made their money by bringing food or coal to the prisoners who could afford to pay. Poor prisoners would have very little food and drink. In fact, the reason many of them were in prison in the first place was for stealing food to feed their families.

Begging for food

Rich prisoners were often sent food and gifts from their
friends and family on the outside. The poor prisoners weren't
so lucky; they didn't have anyone who could afford to send
in extra food. Elizabeth Fry was upset to see these prisoners
leaning through the iron railings of the prison, begging for
money or food from people walking by.

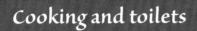

Cooking and toilets

There were no toilets in the Newgate Prison cells, just a bucket in the corner of the room which many people used. Prisoners cooked, washed, slept and used the toilet in the same, overcrowded cell.

Prisoners listen

During one of her visits to Newgate
Prison, Elizabeth Fry began to pray
out loud. A number of women stopped
what they were doing and listened
to her. She was a very confident
and interesting public speaker and,
although some of the prisoners
thought her words were unusual, they
were interested in what she had to say.
Perhaps Elizabeth had learnt how to
speak effectively in public through
listening at Quaker meetings because,
throughout her life, people listened
carefully when Elizabeth spoke.

When Elizabeth saw the effect
she was having on the prisoners
of Newgate, she was spurred on to
dedicate her life to campaigning for
huge changes to the prison system.

3 Time for change

In 1816, Elizabeth Fry asked the female prisoners of Newgate what she could do for them. The prisoners were a huge mix of women. Some were serious criminals who were in prison for violent crimes, and some were women who had stolen food to feed their starving families. But what they had in common was their desire for a prison school. The prisoners wanted to learn and they wanted their children to learn as well.

Elizabeth Fry was determined to open a school for the prisoners. She spent much of her time thinking about the school and how it might work. She wrote in her diary:

> *"I have lately been much occupied in forming a school in Newgate for the children of the poor prisoners as well as the young criminals, which has brought much peace and satisfaction with it ..."*

Elizabeth set about trying to persuade the prison governor to let her run a school. He was reluctant at first and gave many reasons why it was a bad idea.

The reasons the prison governor gave for not opening a school for prisoners

- The women and children were unteachable.
- Their behaviour could not be controlled in a classroom.
- The women were "vicious".
- There was no space.

Elizabeth Fry eventually persuaded the prison governor to give her a small cell to use as a classroom on a trial basis.

Writing new rules

Elizabeth Fry wanted to improve
conditions for prisoners, but
she needed their support. If her
ideas didn't work, then the prison
governor wouldn't let her visits
or the lessons continue. To ensure
the prisoners would support
the changes, Elizabeth Fry
asked them to help her
write new prison rules.

Some of the new prison rules

1. The female prisoners should be looked after by a female matron.

2. The women should be given suitable jobs to keep the prison clean and working smoothly.

3. Some prisoners should be selected as monitors and it is their job to report on anyone breaking the rules.

4. Begging, swearing, arguing and playing cards are all banned.

5. Prisoners should be clean and presentable with washed hands and faces.

The school opens

The first lesson took place in the school with 30 students. Most of these students were children under the age of seven who had been born in prison. However, there were also some adult prisoners who couldn't read. The teacher was a lady called Mary O'Connor who was a prisoner herself, but she'd been educated as a child.

Help is recruited

Elizabeth Fry thought it was important that the prisoners were also taught skills to help them get jobs once they left prison, so she set up sewing classes. Many prisoners were desperate to join the classes. Eventually, the women began sewing items to sell and they were paid a small wage for their work.

Early on in her time at Newgate, Elizabeth realised that reforming prisons was a job that was too big for one person. Elizabeth recruited a group of wealthy women and together they set up The Association for the Improvement of the Female Prisoners in Newgate.

These women took turns to visit Newgate. They raised money to provide food and clothes for the female prisoners and they paid a female matron to be in charge of the women.

Life after prison

When the prison governor visited the women in prison, he was shocked to see them sitting quietly and working hard. He was so impressed that he allowed Elizabeth Fry to set up a more permanent school in the old laundry room.

When the time came for prisoners to be released, Elizabeth Fry and her Association helped the women to find jobs in the hope that reliable, paid work would make them less likely to commit crimes in the future.

A newspaper article from the time shows that Elizabeth Fry and her colleagues raised money to help women settle into life after prison.

> **THE ELIZABETH FRY REFUGE** – The subscription towards the asylum for affording temporary food and shelter to destitute females on their discharge from the metropolitan gaols, now amounts to nearly 5000L. Amongst the subscribers within the last few days are their Majesties the King and Queen of Denmark.
>
> *Morning Post, 4th August 1846*

Did you know?

The symbol for the UK pound (£) is based on the letter "L", an abbreviation for *libra*, the basic Roman unit of weight.

4 The rest of the country and beyond

Elizabeth Fry was pleased with the changes she saw in Newgate Prison, but she was deeply worried about other prisons in the UK. She'd heard stories about other prisoners living in terrible conditions and so she set about travelling around the country visiting as many prisons as she could.

Prison committees

Unusually for the 19th century, Joseph Fry stayed at home to run his business and to look after the children (with the help of his servants). Meanwhile, Elizabeth travelled for her work.

After visiting a prison, Elizabeth would write to the prison governor to thank him and then she would list recommendations on how the prison could be improved. Elizabeth would also approach a rich and influential lady in the area and ask her to run a visiting committee. Elizabeth would also approach a rich and influential lady in the area and ask her to run a visiting committee. This committee was called The Ladies Association and they devoted their time to improving conditions in prisons.

●Aberdeen

Glasgow ●   ●Berwick

Durham ●Newcastle
●

Wakefield ●
●Doncaster

Medical care

The Ladies Association was determined to change prison
rules so that prisoners could be visited by doctors.
Disease and sickness could spread very quickly in prisons due
to the overcrowding and poor hygiene. Elizabeth Fry and her
team believed that if doctors could treat prisoners quickly,
then sickness could be contained and prisoners could remain
healthy enough to continue to work and learn.

Another reason why good medical care was so important
was because of the number of children who lived with their
mothers in prison. Children would only go into prison if there
was no one else to look after them. If their mothers became
sick and died, there would be no one for the children to go to.

Peel's Gaols Act

Elizabeth Fry's work was noticed by important politicians and she was invited to give evidence in the House of Commons in London. At this time, only men were allowed to be politicians so they were shocked when they saw her speak. Some people weren't keen on listening to what she had to say but some were impressed by her passionate and clearly-spoken words. Many of her ideas influenced important laws on how prisons should be run.

Peel's Gaols Act of 1823

In 1823, new rules were written on how prisons should be run.

1. Prisons were to be inspected.
2. Prison guards should be paid a salary and should not sell food to prisoners.
3. Male and female prisoners should be kept separately.
4. Doctors should be allowed to visit prisoners.
5. Prisons should attempt to reform prisoners – this meant that prisons should educate the inmates and help them to live a life without crime.

Work in Europe

Elizabeth wasn't completely happy with the new rules in Peel's Gaols Act as they didn't apply to all prisons. In some cases, the rules made it more difficult for her and her volunteers to visit prisons and see the conditions that prisoners were being kept in, because prison governors were fearful of failing inspections. However, Elizabeth was determined to keep working for change both in and beyond the UK.

News of Elizabeth Fry spread all over Europe. In 1819, two prison reform committees were set up in France. The committees had seen the good work that Elizabeth Fry had done in the UK and they wanted to take her ideas into the French prisons.

34

Meeting royalty

Elizabeth Fry set off on a tour of European prisons. Her name was well-known in many of the countries she visited and she was often invited to dine with important people and even members of the royal family.

Elizabeth Fry meeting King Leopold I of Belgium in 1840

Elizabeth's advice

As stories of Elizabeth's work and knowledge spread further across Europe, she was even sent plans of a **mental health hospital** to be built in Russia. The designer wanted Elizabeth's advice. She sent him a list of suggestions including changing the bars on the windows to iron window frames so as not to upset the patients. Over 18,000 pounds was spent making the changes suggested by Elizabeth which, in the 19th century, was a huge amount of money!

Meeting Queen Victoria

Back in Britain, a young Queen Victoria had heard of Elizabeth Fry and her work, and asked to meet with her. The queen was so impressed by the cause that she donated money to be used to help the female prisoners.

Queen Victoria: a working royal

Queen Victoria and Elizabeth Fry had a lot in common. Dealing with politicians, making important decisions and advising those around them was rarely done by women in the 19th century, but both women were doing exactly that.

5 Transportation

In 1818, Elizabeth Fry heard that the governor of Newgate was expecting the prisoners to riot. Elizabeth rushed down to the prison to find out why.

What is a prison riot?

A prison riot is when many prisoners break the rules all at once. They might fight, shout or destroy prison property. There are always more prisoners than prison guards, so if all the prisoners break the rules at once, it's very difficult for the prison guards to control the violence.

Transportation ships

Despite possible danger, Elizabeth
immediately went to the prisoners
and asked them why they were upset.
They told her that they were being
moved to transportation ships.

The prisoners had heard
stories about how awful
the transportation
ships were. They were to
be moved to the ships in
open carriages and they had
seen members of the public
shouting and throwing things at
prisoners when they were moved.

What was transportation?

Transportation was a punishment handed out to prisoners
instead of the **death penalty**. Prisoners would be shipped
to Australia where they would work on building roads or
another form of hard labour. At the end of their sentence,
ex-prisoners could buy tickets back to the UK. However,
these tickets were very expensive so many ex-prisoners stayed
and made a new life in Australia.

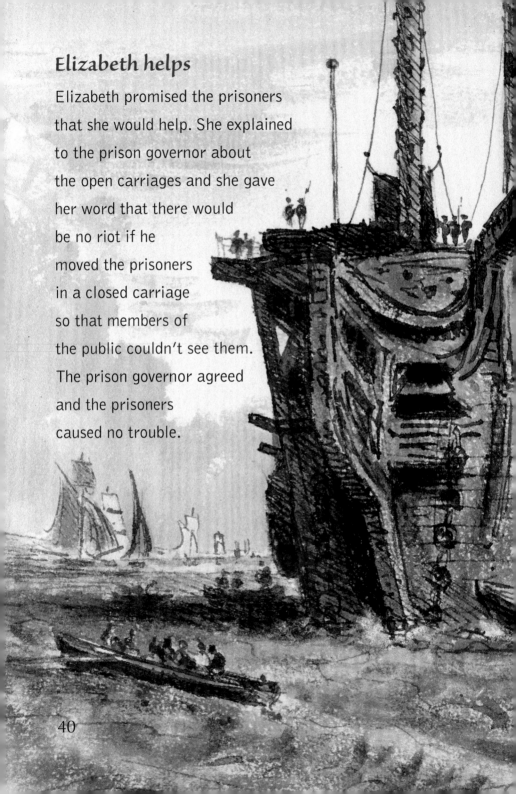

Elizabeth helps

Elizabeth promised the prisoners
that she would help. She explained
to the prison governor about
the open carriages and she gave
her word that there would
be no riot if he
moved the prisoners
in a closed carriage
so that members of
the public couldn't see them.
The prison governor agreed
and the prisoners
caused no trouble.

When the time came for the prisoners
to be moved to the transportation
ship, Elizabeth travelled behind
the carriages and followed
the women on board. Once on
board the ship, Elizabeth Fry
was shocked by what she saw.

What were transportation ships like?

Transportation ships were used firstly to move prisoners from the UK to America and later from the UK to Australia. Prisoners were often kept on board the transportation ships in extremely cramped conditions for weeks or even months. Some were kept in chains for the whole journey. This was very uncomfortable and made moving around difficult.

Often prisoners were kept below deck in the dark. Food could be quite scarce on board and wasn't very healthy. It was very hard to keep clean on board the ships so diseases like typhoid and cholera would spread rapidly. Many prisoners died during the long journey.

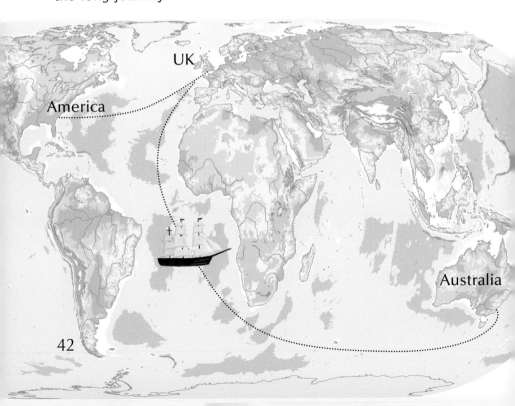

UK

America

Australia

Onboard school

Elizabeth Fry and the Ladies Association immediately
began to campaign for better conditions on board
the transportation ships. They set up a school for the prisoners'
children to attend. They also arranged classes for the adults
who were unable to read or write.

The ship wouldn't leave before it was full so, sometimes,
prisoners would be on board for several weeks before they
set sail. The Ladies Association pleaded with the ship's captain
to allow prisoners to have their chains removed if they were
well behaved and followed all of the rules.

The prisoners from Newgate Prison wanted to continue
working, so scraps of material were gathered and brought
on board. The women continued to sew and make clothes and
they were paid a small amount for their work.

Reluctant listeners

Elizabeth Fry visited the women regularly while they waited in dock and she often read Bible stories to them. There are some reports from the time that suggest the prisoners didn't always like listening to the stories, but Elizabeth Fry's determination to provide better living conditions on board the ship was definitely appreciated.

What she saw on her first visit to a convict ship upset Elizabeth Fry greatly and she spent the next 20 years visiting prisoners on board ships and doing everything she could to make the conditions as bearable as possible.

Mary Wade

Mary Wade was a poor child growing up in London in the late 1700s. When she was 11 years old, she was sentenced to death for stealing. However, while in Newgate Prison, her sentence was changed to transportation and, in 1789, she was on board a ship. Mary Wade, at 13 years of age, is believed to be the youngest person to have been transported. Mary was eventually pardoned for her crime but remained living in Australia. She lived until she was in her eighties and had many children. One of her descendants, Kevin Rudd, became the Prime Minister of Australia in 2007!

Bridewell where Mary Wade was imprisoned

45

6 Criticism of Elizabeth Fry

Today, we can look back on the work of Elizabeth Fry and see how much she improved the lives of prisoners. However, at the time, she was often heavily criticised for the things she said and how she behaved.

Criticism of her work ethic

Joseph and Elizabeth Fry's marriage was very unusual for the 19th century. Elizabeth made her own decisions and didn't ask permission from her husband, as many women were expected to do. As Elizabeth travelled around visiting prisons, Joseph would stay at home with the children and the household. Many people criticised Elizabeth for this. They believed that a mother's job was to stay with the family.

Criticism of her parenting

Several of Elizabeth and Joseph's children were sent away to live with other family members. This was because Joseph's business wasn't doing very well and they needed the children to live elsewhere to save money. However, the family were too proud to admit that they had financial problems so people thought the children had been sent away so that Elizabeth could continue with her work. Some members of the Quaker community and the wider public were critical of Elizabeth for not keeping her children with her.

Criticism of her finances

In 1828, Joseph Fry was declared bankrupt. This meant that he couldn't pay his debts and his business was losing money. Some people were angry and suspicious. They had donated a lot of money to Elizabeth Fry's causes and they were worried that their money had been spent unwisely.

Criticism of her views on the death penalty

Throughout her life, Elizabeth Fry was against the death penalty. She met several women in Newgate Prison who were sentenced to death and she worked tirelessly to try to have their sentences changed to a long prison sentence or to transportation to Australia.

There were around 200 crimes that were punishable by death and some people thought that it was dangerous of Elizabeth to try to change this. They believed that the death penalty was a very complicated matter and not something for women to be involved in. There were many people who still believed that the death penalty was an important part of justice in Britain.

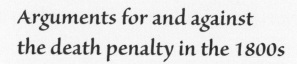

Arguments for and against the death penalty in the 1800s

For

- Harder punishments will stop others from committing crimes.

- Criminals don't deserve sympathy.

- The death penalty helps control the number of people in prisons.

- It's cheaper to sentence someone to death than to keep them in prison.

Against

- Innocent people may be killed.

- It's cruel to take a life and only God should make that decision.

- Young children shouldn't be sentenced to death.

- Some people are only stealing because their families are starving.

49

Criticism of her understanding of poverty

Elizabeth Fry was also criticised for failing to look carefully at the causes of crime. She devoted her life to working with prisoners and she had very strict ideas of what was right and wrong. However, it seemed that she didn't understand that some people had no choice other than to steal. Elizabeth Fry was born into a wealthy family and she married into a wealthy family. She always had a big house with nice things and expensive clothes. Even when Joseph Fry's businesses had failed and he and Elizabeth relied on family members for money, they still kept their house and a small number of servants. Elizabeth Fry was never poor and didn't seem to understand that, for some prisoners, their choice was to either steal food for their family or to watch them starve.

7 Change for good

Before and after Elizabeth Fry

Despite the opposition and criticism, Elizabeth Fry was a huge influence on prison reform in the early 1800s.

before reforms

In the late 1700s, prisons were used purely as a punishment. Prisoners were sent there to serve their time. They were often given hard, boring and pointless jobs. Conditions in prisons were awful and little or no care was given to a prisoner's wellbeing.

after reforms

However, through her campaigns, Elizabeth Fry raised awareness of the prison conditions and demonstrated the positive effect that education and jobs could have on the prisoners. Elizabeth Fry was ahead of her time in suggesting that prisoners should be given paid work. She believed that a job would provide a prisoner with a purpose and motivation. She also believed that prisoners who were able to keep a job would be less likely to reoffend when they were released from prison. This is an idea that's very much part of prisons today.

Five pound note

Elizabeth Fry's influence on the prison system was so important that, from 2002 to 2016, she was pictured on the Bank of England five pound note.

The Bank of England decides who should feature on bank notes, but it's always someone who has made an important contribution to society.

Elizabeth Fry spent all of her life working on behalf of the poor. She did much to help the homeless in both London and Norwich, she campaigned for libraries and schools, she visited mental health hospitals and transportation ships, but it's for her tireless work on prison reform that she'll be remembered.

Glossary

death penalty the legal killing of a person as a punishment for committing a crime

dyslexia a learning difficulty which primarily affects reading and writing skills

mental health hospital a place that cares for and treats people with illnesses of the mind

Plain Quaker a type of Quaker who dresses in plain clothes, leads a simple life and doesn't place importance on material things

spinning a method of producing thread by twisting fibres

Index

Helping the prisoners

Problem

Solution

Prisoners sleep on the floor and wear rags.

Donate clothes to the prisoners.

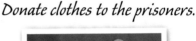

Rich prisoners buy food from prison guards. Poor prisoners are hungry.

Talk to important politicians, asking them to pay prison guards and stop them selling food. Prisons should be inspected to check the food they serve.

Children live in prisons and don't go to school.

Set up a school in the prison.

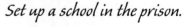

Problem	Solution
Prisoners have no jobs when they leave, so are likely to commit more crimes.	Teach prisoners to sew, to find work once they are released. 
Prisons are dirty. Disease spreads quickly. 	Inspectors to check that prisons are clean. Doctors to visit prisoners to prevent the spread of disease.

Ideas for reading

Written by Gill Matthews
Primary Literacy Consultant

Reading objectives:
- check that the book makes sense to them, discussing their understanding and exploring the meaning of words in context
- summarise the main ideas drawn from more than one paragraph, identifying key details that support the main ideas
- retrieve, record and present information from non-fiction

Spoken language objectives:
- articulate and justify answers, arguments and opinions
- use spoken language to develop understanding through speculating, hypothesising, imagining and exploring ideas

Curriculum links: Citizenship – Preparing to play an active role as citizens

Interest words: influence, contribution, campaigned, tireless

Resources: IT

Build a context for reading

- Ask children to explore the covers of the book and to feedback on what they think the book is about and what they will find out from reading it.
- Discuss the title, asking children what it means to them.
- Focus on the fact that the book is a biography. Ask children what they know about biographies and what features they have.
- Ask what organisational features children think the book might have. Give them time to skim through the book to find the contents, index and glossary. Discuss the purpose and organisation of each of the features.

Understand and apply reading strategies

- Ask children to use the contents page to find the chapter called *Elizabeth Fry's early life*. Read pp2–10 aloud, asking children to make notes of the key points in each section.
- Discuss information that surprised or interested them, encouraging them to support their responses with reasons.